AF480796

THE
Peace of Heaven
JOURNAL

A quiet space to breathe, reflect, and rest in
God's presence. May these pages bring you peace
and gently draw your heart closer to Him.

Be still, and know that I am God.

The Lord blesses His people with peace.

My peace I give you.

My hope comes from Him.

The peace of God will guard your heart and mind.

God is the strength of my heart.

I will give you rest.

Be still, and know that I am God.

The Lord blesses His people with peace.

My peace I give you.

My hope comes from Him.

The peace of God will guard your heart and mind.

God is the strength of my heart.

I will give you rest.

Be still, and know that I am God.

The Lord blesses His people with peace.

My peace I give you.

My hope comes from Him.

The peace of God will guard your heart and mind.

God is the strength of my heart.

I will give you rest.

Be still, and know that I am God.

The Lord blesses His people with peace.

My peace I give you.

My hope comes from Him.

The peace of God will guard your heart and mind.

God is the strength of my heart.

I will give you rest.

Be still, and know that I am God.

The Lord blesses His people with peace.

My peace I give you.

My hope comes from Him.

The peace of God will guard your heart and mind.

God is the strength of my heart.

I will give you rest.

Be still, and know that I am God.

The Lord blesses His people with peace.

My peace I give you.

My hope comes from Him.

The peace of God will guard your heart and mind.

God is the strength of my heart.

I will give you rest.

Be still, and know that I am God.

The Lord blesses His people with peace.

My peace I give you.

My hope comes from Him.

The peace of God will guard your heart and mind.

God is the strength of my heart.

I will give you rest.

Be still, and know that I am God.

The Lord blesses His people with peace.

My peace I give you.

My hope comes from Him.

The peace of God will guard your heart and mind.

God is the strength of my heart.

I will give you rest.

Be still, and know that I am God.

The Lord blesses His people with peace.

My peace I give you.

My hope comes from Him.

The peace of God will guard your heart and mind.

God is the strength of my heart.

I will give you rest.

Be still, and know that I am God.

The Lord blesses His people with peace.

My peace I give you.

My hope comes from Him.

The peace of God will guard your heart and mind.

God is the strength of my heart.

I will give you rest.

Be still, and know that I am God.

The Lord blesses His people with peace.

My peace I give you.

My hope comes from Him.

The peace of God will guard your heart and mind.

God is the strength of my heart.

I will give you rest.

Be still, and know that I am God.

The Lord blesses His people with peace.

My peace I give you.

My hope comes from Him.

The peace of God will guard your heart and mind.

God is the strength of my heart.

I will give you rest.

Be still, and know that I am God.

The Lord blesses His people with peace.

My peace I give you.

My hope comes from Him.

The peace of God will guard your heart and mind.

God is the strength of my heart.

I will give you rest.

Be still, and know that I am God.

The Lord blesses His people with peace.

My peace I give you.

My hope comes from Him.

The peace of God will guard your heart and mind.

God is the strength of my heart.

I will give you rest.

Be still, and know that I am God.

The Lord blesses His people with peace.

My peace I give you.

My hope comes from Him.

The peace of God will guard your heart and mind.

God is the strength of my heart.

I will give you rest.

Be still, and know that I am God.

The Lord blesses His people with peace.

My peace I give you.

My hope comes from Him.

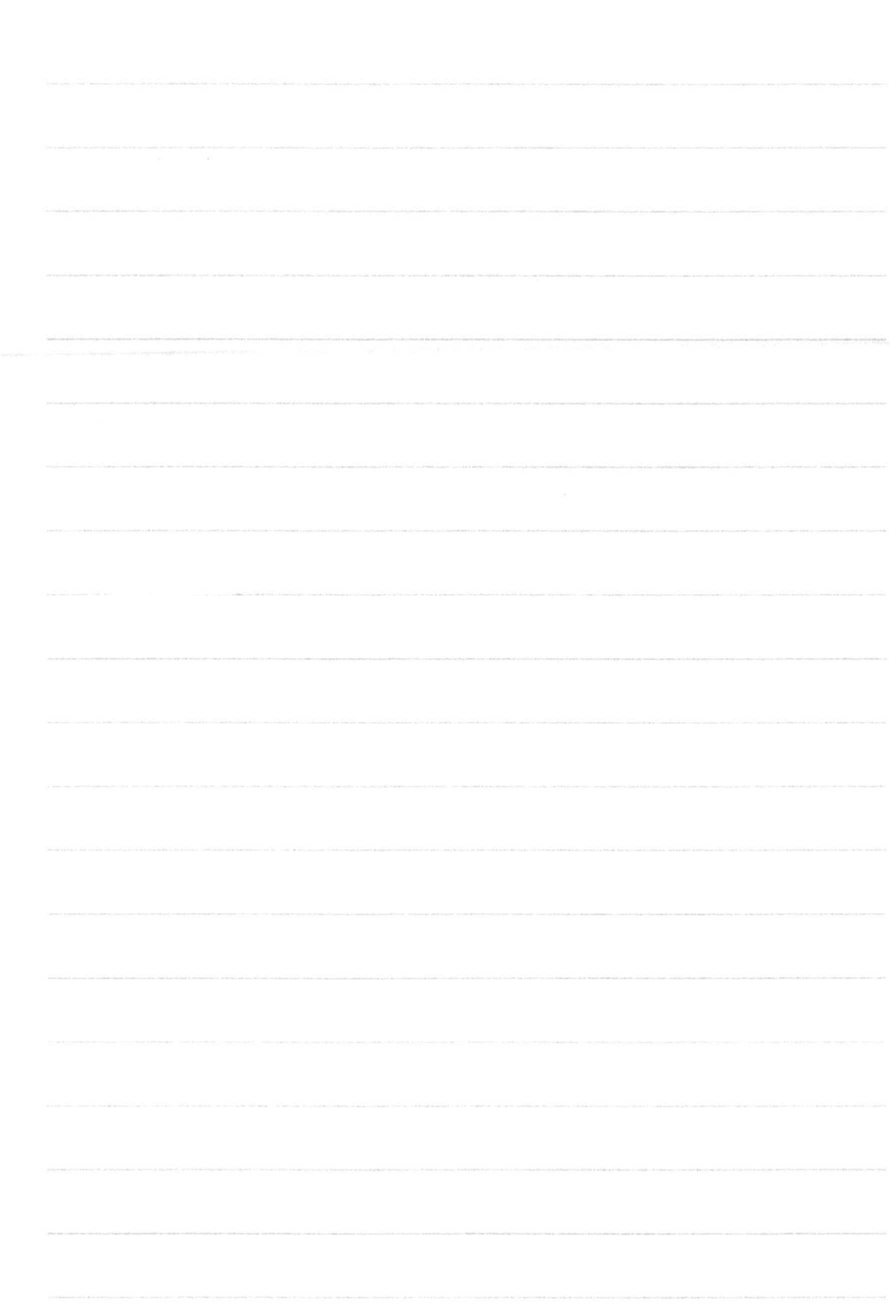

The peace of God will guard your heart and mind.

God is the strength of my heart.

I will give you rest.

Be still, and know that I am God.

The Lord blesses His people with peace.

My peace I give you.

My hope comes from Him.

The peace of God will guard your heart and mind.

God is the strength of my heart.

I will give you rest.

Be still, and know that I am God.

The Lord blesses His people with peace.

My peace I give you.

My hope comes from Him.

The peace of God will guard your heart and mind.

God is the strength of my heart.

I will give you rest.

Be still, and know that I am God.

The Lord blesses His people with peace.

My peace I give you.

My hope comes from Him.

The peace of God will guard your heart and mind.

God is the strength of my heart.

I will give you rest.

Be still, and know that I am God.

The Lord blesses His people with peace.

My peace I give you.

My hope comes from Him.

The peace of God will guard your heart and mind.

God is the strength of my heart.

I will give you rest.

Be still, and know that I am God.

The Lord blesses His people with peace.

My peace I give you.

My hope comes from Him.

The peace of God will guard your heart and mind.

God is the strength of my heart.

I will give you rest.

Be still, and know that I am God.

The Lord blesses His people with peace.

My peace I give you.

My hope comes from Him.

May the peace of heaven meet you in every moment.
You are held. You are loved. You are never alone.

www.ingramcontent.com/pod-product-compliance
Lightning Source LLC
Chambersburg PA
CBHW030900120726
48008CB00002B/61